The Rift Valley

and the Archaeological Evidence of the First Humans

The First Humans and Early Civilizations

The Rift Valley

and the Archaeological Evidence of the First Humans

Kristina Lyn Heitkamp

ROSEN PUBLISHING
New York

Published in 2017 by The Rosen Publishing Group, Inc.
29 East 21st Street, New York, NY 10010

First Edition

Library of Congress Cataloging-in-Publication Data

Names: Heitkamp, Kristina Lyn, author.
Title: The Rift Valley and the archaeological evidence of the first humans / Kristina Lyn Heitkamp.
Description: First edition. | New York : Rosen Pub., 2017. | Series: The first humans and early civilizations | Includes bibliographical references and index.
Identifiers: LCCN 2015049240| ISBN 9781499463200 (library bound) | ISBN 9781499463187 (pbk.) | ISBN 9781499463194 (6-pack)
Subjects: LCSH: Fossil hominids—Great Rift Valley—Juvenile literature. | Prehistoric peoples—Great Rift Valley—Juvenile literature. | Human beings—Origin—Juvenile literature. | Human remains (Archaeology)—Great Rift Valley—Juvenile literature. | Excavations (Archaeology)—Great Rift Valley—Juvenile literature. | Great Rift Valley—Juvenile literature.
Classification: LCC GN282 .H45 2017 | DDC 569.909676—dc23
LC record available at http://lccn.loc.gov/2015049240

Manufactured in China

Contents

INTRODUCTION

A strapping young boy walked along a lake's edge 1.6 million years ago. It was a hot and sunny day in Kenya. Turkana Boy went to the lake to cool off and scavenge for lunch. Unusually tall for his age, he could easily keep a lookout for crocodiles nearby. But today he was distracted. His tooth was killing him. After all, he not brushed them during his nine-and-half-year life.

Turkana Boy fell to his knees and cried out in pain. He reached for his hand ax, wanting to cut out the infected tooth. But he had left his tools at home. Instead he fell face forward into the lake and died. If Turkana Boy had made it to live past nine years old, he could have been more than 6 feet (183 centimeters) tall. But what happened to him?

Usually when we want to learn a story from the past, we go to the source. To study wars, we visit battlefields. We learn about notable leaders through letters or journals. To learn more about your great-great-grandpa Joe, you might look at old black-and-white photos to see that you both share an unruly cowlick and never smile for pictures. Clues can be found in many ways.

But where do you go when you want to learn about something that happened millions of years ago? You go to the bones. To re-create a scene from our ancient past, we look to million-year-old fossils and stone tools. We investigate the earth's sediments and talk to paleoanthropologists, geneticists, and paleoartists. To begin the journey back in time, we start at a

This aerial view of the Rift Valley in Kenya shows the region's variety of landscapes, from rich vegetation to dry desert terrain.

place often called the cradle of humankind. Except this cradle is not like a typical baby bed with stuffed animals and cozy blankets. This cradle can be seen from space. It features volcanoes and hot springs and has the world's largest soda lake. It is also home to a

million or more flamingos. Known as the Grand Canyon of Africa, the Rift Valley is where our story begins.

The Rift Valley is a geological, geographical, and anthropological marvel. Opportunities are endless within the valley. Fossil hunters flock to the area in search of human history. They dig deep to peek into our prehistoric past. Other visitors are attracted to the Rift Valley's promise of adventure, wanting to explore the natural beauty and mystery of the ancient landscape. They climb the highest volcanoes or go on safari in the savannah. The Rift Valley grants storytellers a backdrop for the incredible saga of our historical roots. They imagine what life was like for Turkana Boy and want to solve the mystery of how he died.

Regardless of what inspires us to learn more about the Rift Valley, one thing is certain. It is the one place we all have in common. The Rift Valley is the birthplace of our human story. And this story belongs to each and every one of us.

CHAPTER 1

THE RIFT VALLEY: THE CRADLE OF HUMANKIND

The quest to understand the story of human origins and evolution has long been a source of curiosity. What did our early ancestors look like? What did they eat, and how did they survive? The Rift Valley in Africa has been answering these questions and many more for several decades.

VALLEYS, LAKES, AND VOLCANOES

The Rift Valley is approximately 3,700 miles (5,954 kilometers) in length, about the distance from New York to Juneau, Alaska. It averages 30–40 miles (48–64 km) wide. It stretches north to south, from southwestern Asia to the horn of Africa. Although we tend to think of the Rift Valley as one big valley, it's actually a complex system of rifts and faults that spreads across the area. Several active and semi-active volcanoes, including Mount Kenya and Mount Kilimanjaro, pock the valley. Earthquakes are common along the rift.

A collection of alkaline and freshwater lakes dot the Rift Valley, including the world's largest soda lake, Lake Turkana in northern Kenya. The 155-mile-long

In this photo from 1965, paleoanthropologist Mary Leakey excavates a fossil in Olduvai Gorge.

(249 km) lake sits surrounded by arid desert and grasslands known as the Turkana Basin. Some twenty thousand fossil specimens have been found in the basin and around the lake. Turkana Boy's bones were excavated along the lake's edge.

Other rich fossil sites in the Rift Valley are Olorgesailie, in southern Kenya, and the Olduvai Gorge, in Tanzania. Olorgesailie has been explored since 1942. Several early humans tools, fauna fossils, and even evidence of changing climate have been discovered at the site. From Olorgesailie, it's about a seven-hour drive south to the Olduvai Gorge. A steep-sided ravine, the gorge stretches for 30 miles (48 km) and is close to 300 feet (91 meters) deep. Its sediments have turned up more than sixty hominin fossils. *Hominin* refers to any species that walked upright on two feet and is closely related to humans. Go south another 30 miles (48 km), and you will find yet another fossil goldmine—Laetoli. This site has uncovered important clues to human evolution.

Building the Cradle of Humankind

Although the Rift Valley has been compared to the Grand Canyon in Arizona, it formed differently. The Grand Canyon is a river valley that was shaped by erosion and the Colorado River about one million years ago. The Rift Valley is a massive land depression that was formed by plate tectonics, about twenty-five million years ago.

The Rift Valley sits on three major tectonic plates—the Arabian, Nubian, and Somalian plates. Tectonic plates form the skin of the earth, making up a layer called the lithosphere. Under the lithosphere flows a layer of semi-solid molten rock, called the asthenosphere. The molten rock shifts and moves the plates, either banging them together or pulling them apart. The Rift Valley's three plates are moving away from each other, creating what is called a divergent boundary. As these plates move apart, they form rifts, cliffs, and volcanoes.

The formation of the Rift Valley completely changed Africa's landscape. In less than five million years, East Africa went from flatlands lush with rain forests to mountains, plateaus, and deep rift valleys with several lakes. Very few rift valleys around the world are active. Most are found underwater or have been filled in with sediments and are difficult to explore. The Rift Valley, however, is actively developing. Because it's still moving and rifting, it's a great place to study plate tectonics and a prime location for fossil preservation and recovery.

FOSSIL PRESERVATION AND RECOVERY

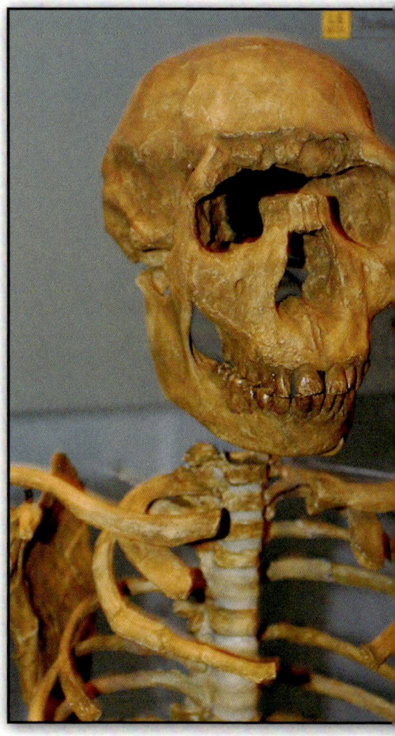

Turkana Boy's skeleton is missing only a few bones, including his hands and feet.

Many years ago, the Rift Valley was abundant with life. Many hominins and other animals lived and died there. Volcanic ash layers, plate tectonics, and sediments have created a perfect storm to preserve their story.

When Turkana Boy died, he likely fell to his death near his namesake, Lake Turkana. When he was discovered, his bones were very well preserved and almost completely intact—a rare find in fossil hunting. Why were his remains so well preserved? As the Rift Valley formed, mountains and highlands were cut from the land. Hominins who perished in the lower lands, like Turkana Boy, would quickly be buried by rainwater and sediment runoff from the highlands. This created an ideal burial and preservation ground.

DOWN IN THE DIRT

Imagine walking for hours along lunar-like landscapes in temperatures of more than 100° F (37° C). Your head is down, your eyes probing every rock, pebble, and crevice in hopes of finding something, anything, in the dry, cracked earth. Scrambling down stale air gullies, searching and scanning. Fossil hunting is grueling work. But the anticipation of possible discoveries propels the exploration.

When paleoanthropologist Donald Johanson found the groundbreaking fossil Lucy, he was on his way back to camp after a long, hot morning of fossil hunting. He happened to look over his shoulder, when he spotted a fragment of bone—Lucy's knee. Perseverance, patience, and a trained eye are all key to finding landmark fossils in the Rift Valley. And don't forget to always look over your shoulder!

After cautiously excavating the pieces, each bone fragment is taken back to camp to be carefully cleaned and put together. Assembling the hundreds of pieces, some of which are miniscule, is both time consuming and labor intensive. When the fossils are finally put together, we get a closer look at life millions of years ago. The bones begin to tell stories of their own, like how these beings moved around or even how they died.

Seasonal flooding and fluctuating lake levels also aided in the proper burial of bones.

Volcano eruptions were a part of life in the Rift Valley. When the active mountaintops rained ash, layers of the hard mineral dust would settle on top of artifacts. Unlike wood-burning ash, volcanic ash is firm and doesn't dissolve in water. Along with mud, clay, and sediments, volcanic ash helped to bury and protect bones.

It's one thing to preserve fossils, but it's another to actually find them. Suppose a fossil is buried under several feet of rock and dirt. It can be difficult to know where a fossil might be found. Because the Rift Valley is still active, the eroding highlands help to push up new layers of earth begging to be excavated.

CLIMATE IN THE VALLEY

The Rift Valley is also important for understanding the origins of human evolution. Because many different types hominin fossils have been found along the rift, it is important to look at the evolution of the land and to determine what influence the climate had on our ancient ancestors.

The Olorgesailie site in southern Kenya has proven to be an excellent source of climate clues because it is a great place to dig deep. Here paleoanthropologists have replaced their chisels and brushes with deep-earth digging drills. In a southern region of

This view of the Rift Valley is from the Kamandura Mai-mahiu Narok Road in Kenya. The valley is a mix of highlands and lowlands of diverse terrain and climates.

Olorgesailie, scientists have tunneled more than 500 feet (152 m) down to extract ancient sediment layers. This creates cores of earth. Each core is examined in 5-foot (1.5-m) sections. Centimeter by centimeter, paleoanthropologists inspect the plastic-packaged prehistoric rock. With this method, they can look back thousands or millions of years ago to see records of rainfall, temperature, vegetation, and even environmental pressures. Clues point to years of active volcanic eruptions alternating with quiet lake phases and dry periods. Like flipping through a family photo album, paleoanthropologists can get a glimpse of the changing faces of the Rift Valley. The fluctuating weather and environmental pressures could have forced our early ancestors to evolve, adapting to the shifting landscape.

Chapter 2
The Many Faces of Hominins

For several years, early human evolution has been thought of as one long epic story—species after species slowly evolving into the next, like the iconic image of a hairy, knuckle-walking ape turning into a hairless, upright walking human. But as it turns out, that's not the case at all. Gone is the linear line of evolution. We now know that three or four different early human species lived at the same time. To help understand the complexity of the prehistoric past, paleoanthropologists place our early human ancestors into a family tree.

Our Big Family Tree

Classifying, or grouping, helps us to better understand the relationships between different early human species. The hominin family can be divided into four main groups (each called a genus) that can then be broken down further into different species. The groups are *Ardipithecus*, *Australopithecus*, *Paranthropus*, and *Homo*.

The *Ardipithecus* group is the species of earliest humans. They lived in eastern Africa from around seven million to four million years ago. Close in size to chimps, they weren't very tall. They ate mostly fruits, nuts, and

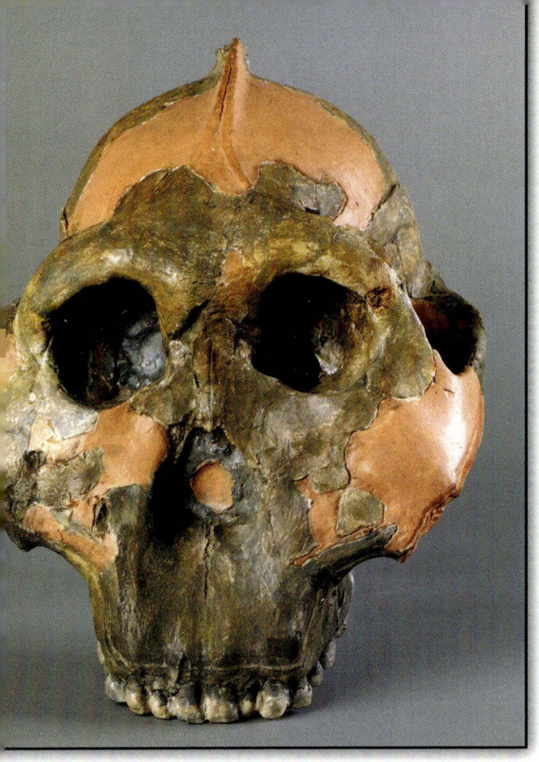

Note the small braincase and flaring cheekbones in this careful reconstruction of a Paranthropus boisei *skull.*

plants. *Ardipithecus* evolved in Africa and is our closest link to other primates. More than one hundred specimens have been found in the Rift Valley. Although they had many ape-like traits, such as longer arms and curved fingers for climbing, they also had key human features, such as smaller canines and evidence of bipedalism. Bipedalism means habitually walking upright on two feet. Evidence of bipedalism can include an arched foot, a broad pelvis, thighbones that angle in toward the knees, and a central-positioned opening for the spinal cord to attach to the skull. These features help bear the weight and balance of upright walking.

Another species group that also showed evidence of bipedalism is *Australopithecus*. They lived between four million and two million years ago. Still a lot shorter than average humans today, *Australopithecus* males averaged 4 feet 6 inches (138 cm), and females averaged 3 feet 9 inches (115 cm). Their diet consisted of plants and fruits. More than three hundred individual

Australopithecus have been found in the Rift Valley. They were a pretty successful species, living more than nine hundred thousand years.

The *Paranthropus* group lived at the same time as the *Australopithecus* group, possibly even living side by side in the Rift Valley. They lived between 2.7 million to 1.2 million years ago. They were about the same height as *Australopithecus*, but their bodies were heavier and more robust. They also had massive jaw muscles designed for heavy chewing. What exactly they chomped on, researchers are still trying to figure out.

The species group we are most familiar with is the *Homo* genus. Just like the other groups, it contains several species. These include *Homo habilis*, *Homo erectus*, *Homo neanderthalensis*, and *Homo sapiens*—our own species. The oldest *Homo* species is *Homo rudolfensis*, living between 1.9 and 1.8 million years ago. *Homo sapiens* are the only surviving *Homo* species, living for last two hundred thousand years. The *Homo* genus had longer legs for running, lighter builds, bigger brains, and smaller teeth. *Homo erectus* is thought to be the first *Homo* species to have expanded outside of Africa. *Homo neanderthalensis* is our closest extinct human relative. Researchers are still debating and exploring the relationships and connections between all the different *Homo* genus species.

erectus

Significant Fossil Finds

Early human fossils are difficult to find. Discovering a skeleton is like striking gold. Hominin bones help piece together our ancient history. Below are a few of the notable finds to date, but paleoanthropologists are still digging.

In 1994, paleoanthropologist Tim White and his team found an almost complete *Ardipithecus*

Homo erectus *had modern human-like body proportions and could grow up to 6 feet (182 cm) tall.*

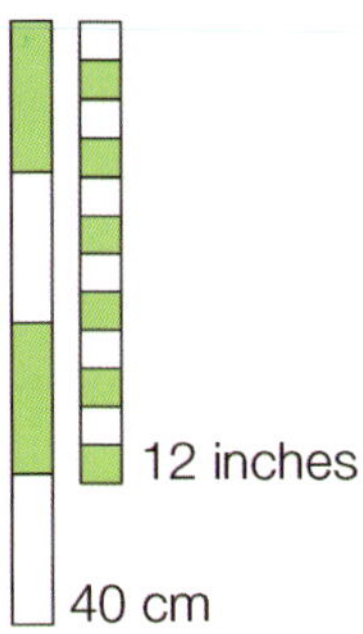

Relative or Ancestor?

The difference between a relative and ancestor can be a little confusing. Our relatives are not our ancestors. Think of it like this: your great-great-grandma is an ancestor, but your aunt is a relative. A relative is a family member that may share some DNA with you, but you did not descend from him or her. An ancestor is a family member that shares DNA with you and who is linked to your creation. You are descended from an ancestor, but not a relative. Modern humans share some DNA with gorillas and chimps, but the hairy primates are relatives, not ancestors. Apes and humans descended from a common ancestor that lived between eight and six million years ago.

ramidus in Gona, Ethiopia. They named the 4.4-million-year-old female skeleton Ardi. She had long arms with flexible wrists and hands, which shows that she was bipedal and not a knuckle-walker. To be a knuckle-walker, the hands and wrists have to be super stiff in order to bear the weight of the walk. Ardi also had a chimp-size brain and an opposable big toe for grasping objects or branches with her feet. Thousand of fossils have since been discovered in the same site, including

A paleoartist recreated this rendering of the Australopithecus *Lucy. She was fully grown at 3.6 feet (110 cm) tall.*

fossilized wood and seeds. This evidence shows that Ardi lived in a wooded habitat.

Named after the Beatles' song "Lucy in the Sky with Diamonds," Lucy was discovered by American paleoanthropologist Donald Johanson in 1974, in Hadar, Ethiopia. Johanson has been digging for fossils for many years and has greatly contributed to the study of human origins. His Lucy fossil has become a benchmark for other fossil finds. After two weeks of excavations, 40 percent of her skeleton was unearthed. She is *Australopithecus afarensis* and is about three million years old. Lucy walked upright and had a smaller brain, and her skeleton shows evidence for a convergent big toe—the big toe was in line with the rest, unlike Ardi's opposable big toe.

Lucy's Baby was found a few miles south of Lucy. But technically this young *Australopithecus* was not Lucy's child because she is 3.3 million years old. The fossilized toddler was only three years old when she died. Her legs indicate that she was bipedal, but her curved fingers signify that she also tree-climbed. Lucy's Baby is the world's oldest child found to date.

Another *Australopithecus* that faced his death in toddlerhood is the Taung Child. He was uncovered by local quarrymen in Taung, South Africa, in 1924. His fossil is about 2.8 million years old. Some researchers think an eagle killed him. His skull was found with puncture marks around his eye sockets and talon claw marks scratched on his cranium. Eggshells were also uncovered at the site. Taung Child was one of the first early human fossils found in Africa.

Legendary paleoanthropologist Richard Leakey found his first fossil when he was only six years old.

Another fossil find in the Rift Valley is the Black Skull. Alan Walker discovered this 2.5-million-year-old skull from the group *Paranthropus* in West Turkana, Kenya, in 1985. Black skull got his name from the black coloration of his skull after sitting in manganese-rich soil for millions of years.

Discovered in 1984 by famous fossil chaser Kamoya Kimeu in West Turkana, Kenya, Turkana Boy is a 1.6-million-year-old *Homo erectus*. As we know, he may have suffered from horrific tooth pain. Evidence in his jaw shows he had an abscessed tooth that could

The Millennium Man

Discovered in 2001 by French paleontologist Brigitte Senut and French geologist Martin Pickford in central Kenya, *Orrorin tugenensis* is a six-million-year-old species in the *Ardipithecus* group. Their team found more than a dozen fossils, including a partial femur, bits of a lower jaw, and several teeth. This early hominin fossil offers a new combination of ape and human traits. But paleoanthropologists are still trying to figure if he's a direct human ancestor and if he was bipedal. The Millennium Man is a candidate for the title of earliest human.

have caused an infection that led to his death. Another notable *Homo* genus find, and contender for the oldest *Homo sapiens* fossil, is Omo I. Discovered in 1967 by Kenyan paleoanthropologist Richard Leakey in Omo River, Ethiopia, Omo I is 195,000 years old. The fossil skull has several trademarks of modern humanness, including a flat face, high forehead, round braincase, and fully formed chin. Since his discovery, the well-know fossil hunter Leakey has continued to enrich the knowledge of human evolution and education.

The Bigger Picture

All of these discoveries are just the tip of the iceberg of fossils found over the years and that continue to be uncovered today. From knobby knee bones to smaller canines, early human fossils have been discovered all throughout the Rift Valley, as well as in other parts of Africa. With this evidence, paleoanthropologists have pieced together what life was like for a whole host of hominins.

Chapter 3

Reading the Clues Left Behind

For several million years, hominins lived and died in the Rift Valley. Paleoanthropologists learn what life was like by the artifacts they left behind. They can find out what they ate, what animals shared their habitat, and how they managed survival in a changing landscape.

One Small Step, One Step for Humankind

Finding early human fossils is always a treat. But finding evidence of behavior is like discovering that your dog can walk upright. In 1978, a team of scientists led by Mary Leakey (Richard's mom) and Paul Abell found evidence of bipedalism. They discovered a path of seventy early human footprints in Laetoli, Tanzania. The 88-foot-long (27 m) footprint trail has been named the Laetoli footprints.

In Laetoli 3.6 million years ago, a nearby volcano called Sadiman erupted, leaving a layer of ash in its wake. Soon after, a storm rolled through. When the rainwater mixed with the ash, it created an impressionable surface, almost like wet cement. Then inhabitants in the area, including birds and at least two hominins, walked along the surface, leaving behind their prints. Sadiman erupted once more, dropping another layer of ash, sealing in the prints. The combination of a volcanic eruption, a rainstorm, and another ash fall all helped preserve the prints.

After scientists studied them, the Laetoli footprints were reburied to keep them preserved.

Paleoanthropologists believe that a member of the genus *Australopithecus*, Lucy's group, made the prints. Previous fossils found have proved evidence of bipedalism, but the prints show behavior—something bones can't show. Lucy's species walked with a short stride and moved the way modern humans do with a heel-strike followed by a toe-off step.

Good Eats in the Rift

Our early ancestors couldn't just stroll down to a local grocery store for milk and bread, so what did they eat? That ranges from fruits and nuts to meat and even wood. Scientists find clues to their diet deep inside fossil mouths. They look to the teeth.

Ardipithecus, Ardi's genus, most likely were omnivores. They ate a diet of plants, meat, and fruit. Examining teeth, researchers look at the tooth's enamel. Thick enamel points to a diet of tough, abrasive food like nuts and tubers. Thin enamel shows a diet of softer foods like fruit. The enamel on Ardi's teeth was not very thick, nor was it very thin. Instead the teeth had a combination similar to our own that suggests she had a mixed diet. Her incisors had a wear pattern that showed she was not a specialized frugivore (fruit eater), although she may have avoided hard foods.

Australopithecus, Lucy's genus, had a robust jaw and teeth that could grind hard foods. But she often preferred softer foods like plants and fruit. However, when vegetation was sparse, and because she had strong teeth, she could forage on other things—like wood. Plaque found on an *Australopithecus sediba*'s teeth shows evidence of meals of grasses, fruit, and even bark or wood.

Paranthropus, often called the Nutcracker because of its massive molars and huge jaw and muscles, probably kept its mouth packed with hard nuts, seeds, and tubers. But tiny scratches found on *Paranthropus* teeth show evidence that these hominins mostly dined on soft fruits and insects.

Members of the *Homo* genus, such as Turkana Boy, had much smaller teeth than *Paranthropus* and

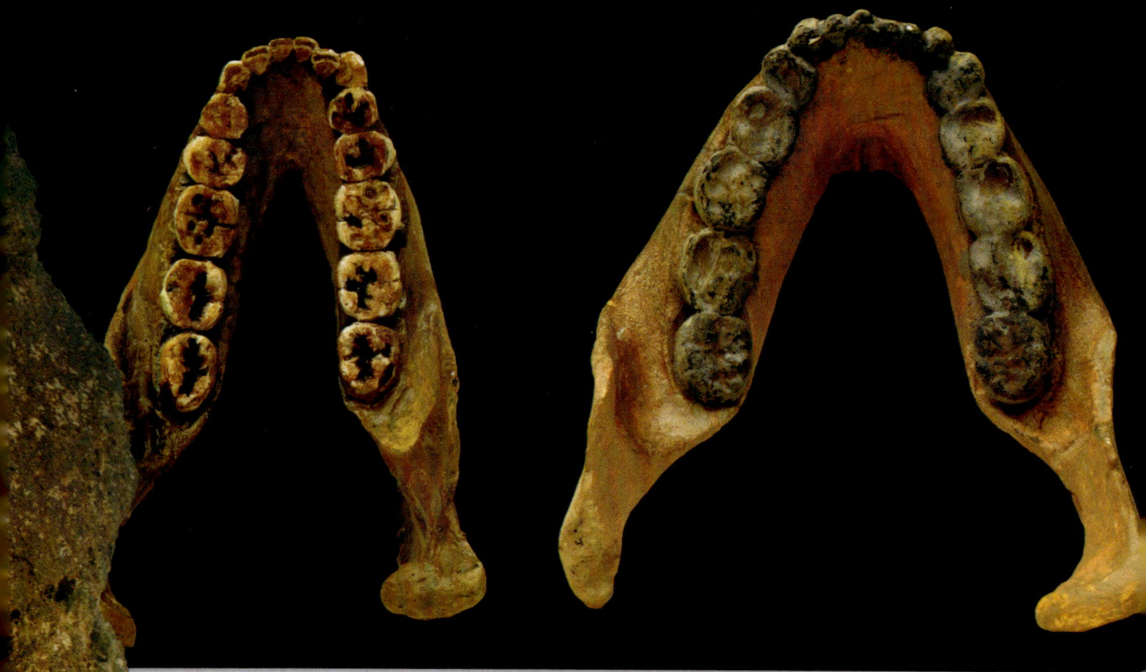

These are lower jaw casts of Paranthropus robustus *and* Paranthropus boisei. *Their teeth were four times the size of modern human's teeth.*

Australopithecus. They had a flexible and adaptable diet. Turkana Boy's tooth enamel was thick and his jaw strong, so he could chew on hard foods like woody plants and animal meat. But his dental wear shows he didn't just eat tough foods. He ate a diverse diet of leaves, fruits, and meats. Turkana Boy likely did not eat alone either. A nine hundred thousand-year-old elephant butchery site was discovered in Olorgesailie, Tanzania. Researchers found cut marks on the elephant's bones, indicating where the meat and marrow were scrapped and cut away. More than twenty-three hundred stone tools were excavated near the ancient elephant's skeleton. Zebra and antelope butchery sites were also uncovered in neighboring areas.

Dinner Partners or Dinner?

Early humans shared their habitat with many other animals. Some of these animals coexisted with hominins, harmlessly sharing water holes and vegetation grub. Others may have been predators and dangerously competed for domination and survival.

Among fauna fossils found, monkeys, hippos, and wild pigs were abundant. Weighing close to 185 pounds (83 kilograms), the Gelada baboon is the largest monkey species ever recorded in history. It lived in the Rift Valley between one million and seven hundred thousand years ago but went extinct in Africa about six hundred thousand years ago. Another big animal that lived with our early ancestors was the *Hippopotamus gorgops*. This hippo was a lot larger than modern hippos. It weighed up to 9,900 pounds (4,490 kg) and was almost 7 feet (213 cm) tall. Its footprints are found in many places where early humans liked to visit, too. About the size of small hippos, wild pigs were also a part of the landscape. Much bigger than today's warthog, this wild pig ate lots of grasses and lived in the Rift Valley about one million ago. As the environment shifted, between 900,000 and 360,000 years ago, these species of animals went extinct and were replaced with smaller and more adaptable relatives.

Early humans also shared the land with predators. Without claws or razor-sharp teeth, hominins had to try

Methods of Dating

After a long, sweaty day of fossil hunting in the Rift Valley, you finally find a partial skull. You high-five your teammates! But before the celebration commences, you remember the fossil must be dated. Is it an undiscovered hominin species or is it a previous fossil hunter who perished from heatstroke? There are some well-tested methods of dating fossils.

Thermo-luminescence and electron spin resonance measure time passed by looking at the electrons that were absorbed and got stuck in the fossil. These methods can be used to date human teeth, seashells, and rocks. Potassium-argon, radiocarbon, and argon-argon dating are used to date million-year-old minerals. These methods measure how much radioactive decay is left over and are best at dating really old fossils. A method that has been used since the 1960s, paleomagnetism dating compares earth's magnetic field to the magnetic particles found in the sediments where a fossil was unearthed. For excavation sites from which scientists can't quite get an accurate date on the sediments, they use the biochronology method. They will compare the fauna fossils found to well-dated species from other sites. A million-year-old hyena found in Olorgesailie can help date a hyena found in another site.

to keep safe. Many hominin fossils have been discovered with skullcaps pierced with cougar canine holes. Others have talon scratches and puncture holes like those found on the Taung Child. Even early human leg bones have been found with the ends chewed and gnawed down to a nub.

Australopithecus afarensis *walked upright, but its long arms suggest that it lived both in trees and on the ground.*

Changing Climate, Changing Behavior

Earth's environment has shifted between warm and cool climates over the past ten million years. How did early humans adapt and survive the environmental changes, especially severe weather like monsoons, extreme droughts, and volcanic eruptions? They adapted for survival. They became bipedal and social. They sought shade from the extreme heat. They found safer places to inhabit.

Exactly when bipedalism occurred or what provoked it is still debated and explored. At some point in the past, early humans shifted from ape-like walking to walking upright and eventually running. Even though they walked instead of swinging from branches, hominins still stayed close to trees. To survive extreme heat, they hunted for shade. Stone tools have been found around remnants of old tree stumps and roots, showing that hominins used the shade of large trees for survival. Another survival technique was to seek out higher ground. Some researchers believe the locations where hominins died show that they sought refuge in highland areas for protection from floods and roving predators. Eating well also played an important role in survival. Finding food, especially meat, can be challenging as a solo mission. Elephant, zebra, and antelope butchery sites show evidence of social eating and sharing.

Chapter 4
Tools and Things

Stone tools, hearths, and prehistoric art all provide evidence of how early humans interacted with their environment and each other. The artifacts illustrate how they evolved from passive animals to active hominins shaping and communicating with their environment.

Users and Producers

We use computers, but most of us haven't actually built a computer. Early humans had been utilizing tools for millions of years, but they developed toolmaking later. From using a rock to pound nuts to shaping that rock to cut meat from a bone to then using that bone to create a projectile point for spear hunting—all are major stepping-stones to becoming human. When analyzing ancient tools, researchers will look for the hand of a human, to see if it was just used or if it was produced to better serve its user.

The Evolution of Tools

As archaeological sites in the Rift Valley have been excavated, several kinds of stone tools have been found. These tools offer evidence of hominin behavior, mental ability, and the evolution of industry.

Animals and Their Tools

Scientists once thought that the ability to use tools set hominins apart from the rest of the animal kingdom. Well, it turns out several other animals employ tools, too, and in cool and unexpected ways.

Crows will prune a branch and then poke it in a hole to retrieve an edible treat. These cunning corvids will also drop stones in water to raise the water level to push a tasty treat to the surface. Like crows, chimps will also fashion a stick into a specialized tool for foraging for army ants or dipping for honey. One of the smartest animals in the world, elephants will solve problems with tools. They will custom fly swatters out of branches. They will even dig up watering holes with their massive feet and then stuff balls of chewed bark into the water pit to keep it safe. Another crafty one is the dolphin. They can hunt with tools, much like humans. Using sea sponges on their noses, some of these clever cetaceans will forage for food along the seafloor, stirring up the sand and hidden fish.

First discovered in Olduvai Gorge in Tanzania, Oldowan tools date between 2.6 and 1.2 million years old. The Oldowan stone toolkit includes hammerstones, choppers, and scrappers. Hammerstones are handheld stones that were used to crush nuts,

Oldowan stone chopping tools show a variety of shapes and sizes with sharp edges used for preparing food.

tubers, and other plant food. They were also used to create choppers. Hominins would strike one hammerstone against another stone to create a sharp edge. Choppers were used to cut meat and marrow from bones. Taking a closer look at choppers, evidence shows they were also used for cutting plants. Scrappers were the larger pieces of stone flakes that fell off when making the choppers. Scrappers were also used to clean meat off bones.

Soon tools became more intentional. The Oldowan toolkit was replaced with the Acheulean toolkit. This kit included hand axes. Many hand axes have been found at the Olorgesailie site dating between 1.2 million and 900,000 years old. Early humans used local rocks to make tools—including fourteen different types of volcanic rock—testing to see which stone worked best. Hand axes were used for over a million years, until two hundred thousand years ago. After perfecting the hand ax, early humans began to make smaller and more precise tools. They took longer to make, but hominins could travel with the smaller tools while searching for food or visiting other groups. Acheulean toolkits have been found in Africa, Asia, Europe, and the Middle East.

The latest in tool discovery is still being investigated. Along the western shore of Lake Turkana in the Rift Valley, a team of scientists found stone tools dating around 3.3 million years old. This suggests that members of the *Australopithecus*, Lucy's genus, could have have been the first early humans to make tools, bumping out *Homo habilis* for the first toolmaker.

The Lomekwi tools are much larger and more primitive than Oldowan tools. However, no hominin fossils or cutmarked bones were found at the site, so scientists are still unsure who used the tools and for what purpose.

CHUNKY CRAYONS AND CROSSHATCH

Prehistoric art is more than just doodles on a rock wall. It's an ancient form of communication and expression. It predates writing of any kind and is a real treasure when found.

In 1996, Larry Barham discovered ancient pigments in Twin Rivers, Zambia. He found hundreds of the colorful rocks in red, brown, pink, purple, yellow, and blue. Several of the pieces showed evidence

This block of red ocher with an intentional etched design was found in Blombos Cave. The piece is 2.3 inches (6 cm) long, about the size of a rubber eraser.

of grinding or rubbing. They may have been used like crayons to paint cave walls or ground down to paste for body painting. The chunky crayons are about 250,000 years old.

In 2002, another incredible treasure was discovered in a cave on the coast of southern Africa. Inside the Blombos Cave, paleoanthropologists found an ocher plaque marked with crosshatch strokes. Some researchers believe the etchings may be an ancient code or counting marks. The plaque could be evidence of early symbolic thinking. It's dated about seventy-seven thousand years old. Another find in the seaside cave were clusters of Nassarius shell. The shells have holes punched through, indicating they may have been strung as beads and worn. Researchers propose that wearing shell jewelry represented a person's group, age, sex, or even social status.

Named after the first spacecraft to land on the moon, the Apollo 11 Plaque is anything but moon rock. In 1969, the stone slab was found in a cave in Zambia. It has been dated between sixty thousand and forty thousand years old. The artist used charcoal to paint what looks like an animal hybrid—part man and part cat or zebra. But it's hard to determine. Several other painted slabs of rock were also found in the cave.

What's Cooking?

Evidence found of modern behavior indicates that early humans may have been thinking in ways that scientists originally thought they were not capable of. Hominins were not only becoming more anatomically modern but they also started to develop critical modern behaviors, like using symbols and controlling fire.

Some researchers think that cooking with fire reaches back more than 1.5 million years ago. But the earliest hearths found are 790,000 years old. A hearth is a firepit that is lined with stones, used for cooking, heating, socializing, making tools, and even warding off predators. A cave in South Africa has provided clues that fire control could have happened one million years ago. Inside the Wonderwerk Cave, archaeologists excavated several signs of fire use, including

The excavation sites inside the Wonderwerk Cave have uncovered rock art, stone tools, and evidence of fire use. Paleoanthropologists have been digging in the massive cave since the 1940s.

tiny charred bones, ash from burned twigs and grasses, and probable hearths. This evidence helps to support the cooking hypothesis developed by Richard Wrangham of Harvard University. According to his theory, *Homo erectus* cooked with fire around 1.9 million years ago. He says the ability to control fire and cook food helped the *Homo* genus evolve into modern man. With this new source of energy-rich cooked protein, their brains expanded. Their bodies grew taller. Teeth became smaller because cooked food allowed for easier chewing and digestion. Before the finds in the Wonderwerk Cave, the oldest evidence of fire control came from Gesher Benot-Ya'aqov, Israel. Researchers found fire-altered stone tools, burned fruit, and wood dating back 790,000 years. However, several other sites are still being investigated for ancient fire use.

Chapter 5

Out of Africa

Although the Rift Valley has been an abundant source of fossils, other hominin bones and artifacts have been discovered outside the cradle of humankind. Evidence found proves that early human evolution and migration is complex. Paleoanthropologists continue to find new pieces of the puzzle.

Million-Year-Old Club

Just hop across the Indian Ocean from Africa to Indonesia and you will find the ancient site of Java Man. In 1891, Dutch physician Dr. Eugène Dubois was anxious to discover an ancestral missing link. Instead he found Java Man, a *Homo erectus* dated between one million and seven hundred thousand years old. Dr. Dubois found a partial skullcap, three teeth, and a femur. Java Man had a smaller brain, flat forehead, and distinct browridges.

Also joining the million-year-old club are the Dmanisi skulls found in Dmanisi in the country of Georgia. Beginning excavations in 1999, researchers led by David Lordkipanidze have so far found a total of five *Homo erectus* skulls on the site. The fossils have an interesting combination of *Homo* ge-

This toothless skull is one of the five found in Dmanisi, in the Republic of Georgia.

nus features, like the long face of a *Homo erectus* and a small brain like *Homo habilis*. One of the Dmanisi skulls was found without any teeth. Long before his death, most of his teeth had fallen out and his jaw had deteriorated. It is likely that members of his social group or family took care of him, showing early evidence of compassion. The Dmanisi skulls are some of the earliest skulls known outside of Africa, dated 1.77 million years old.

ALMOST MILLION-YEAR-OLD CLUB

Other noteworthy ancient fossils have been discovered across China, Israel, and France. Found in a cave at Zhoukoudian, China, the Peking man was the first *Homo erectus* uncovered in China. His skullcap was found in 1927. Later excavations turned up other partial skulls. The bones are dated between 780,000 and 400,000 years old. The skullcap has the usual *Homo* genus characteristics: a small forehead,

Piltdown Man: The Faked Missing Link

What has an orangutan jaw, a six-hundred-year-old human cranium, and a chimpanzee tooth? The Piltdown man—one of the biggest hoaxes exposed in the world of paleoanthropology.

In 1912, early human fossils were found in a gravel pit at Piltdown Common, in southern England. The nine-piece set included a mandible, skull fragments, and teeth. Piltdown man was the first hominin found in England and was believed to be the missing link between apes and humans. The discovery was met with mixed reviews. But it wasn't until almost fifty years later when it was determined that the Piltdown man was a fake.

A closer look revealed the pieces actually came from different species—a modern human, a chimp, and an orangutan. The teeth had been filed down. Chemical tests proved that the bone pieces had been deliberately stained to look old. Carbon dating confirmed the age of the human skull. The proof was in the pudding. Piltdown Man was a fake. But the culprit is still unknown. Some say it was the amateur archaeologist Charles Dawson who found and announced the fake fossil. He had been known to cry wolf a few times before. Some point a finger to others who also claimed the find, including a Jesuit priest, an anatomist, and a British museum volunteer. However, the mystery still remains.

Created by French sculptor Elisabeth Daynès, this reconstruction of a Cro-Magon hunter is based on seventeen thousand-year-old fossils found in southwestern France.

a heavy browridge, and a chinless jaw. His teeth were also smaller and more modern. Unfortunately, the fossils disappeared in 1941 while en route to the United States from China for safekeeping during World War II. Luckily fossil casts and detailed descriptions were made and kept. The cave in Qafzeh, Israel, where R. Neuville unearthed fifteen early *Homo* genus fossils in 1933 is almost 4,000 miles (6,440 km) west from China. Along with the bones, seventy-one pieces of red ocher and ocher-stained stone tools were found indicating the cave may have been an intentional burial site. The fossils are dated one hundred thousand years old.

Head northwest another 3,000 miles (4,830 km) from Israel to southwestern France to find the excavation site of the first ancient *Homo sapiens* fossil discovered; thirty thousand-year-old Cro-Magnon 1 was found in 1868 in a rock shelter. Digging deeper into the shallow cave, researchers unearthed more fossils—a total of four adults, one infant, and other bone fragments. The skeletons appeared to have suffered from physical ailments, including a fungal infection, a skull fracture, and an unknown traumatic injury. It's thought that this group of Cro-Magnons (as early *Homo sapiens* in Europe are sometimes called) cared for and supported one another. Researchers also discovered animal teeth pendants and necklaces. There was even prehistoric art scribed on the cave walls. Anthropologists believe the rock shelter to be an ancient burial site. Burial rituals of the dead signify a change toward modern behavior.

Migration and Evolution

For several millions of years, early humans evolved and survived in Africa. About two million years ago they begin to journey to other parts of the world. The fossils found have helped paleoanthropologists determine early human origins and a migration path throughout the world. The route probably began with a trek from Africa to Asia, between 2 million and 1.8 million years ago. A little later, between 1.5 million and 1 million years ago, they migrated to Europe. Modern humans made their way to Australia within the past sixty thousand years and to the Americas about thirty thousand years ago. But the jury is still out on exactly what motivated early humans to migrate and why they went to specific places.

Home Turf: Kennewick Man and Arlington Springs Man

During the summer of 1996, two college kids found a human skull along a bank of the Columbia River in Kennewick, Washington. Unsure if they stumbled upon a crime scene or something dangerous, they called the police. The police called a coroner, and the coroner called local archaeologist James Chatters. Using radiocarbon dating, Kennewick Man is dated about nine thousand years old. This makes him one of the oldest complete *Homo sapiens* skeletons found in North America. His teeth were cavity-free and worn down to the root, indicating he

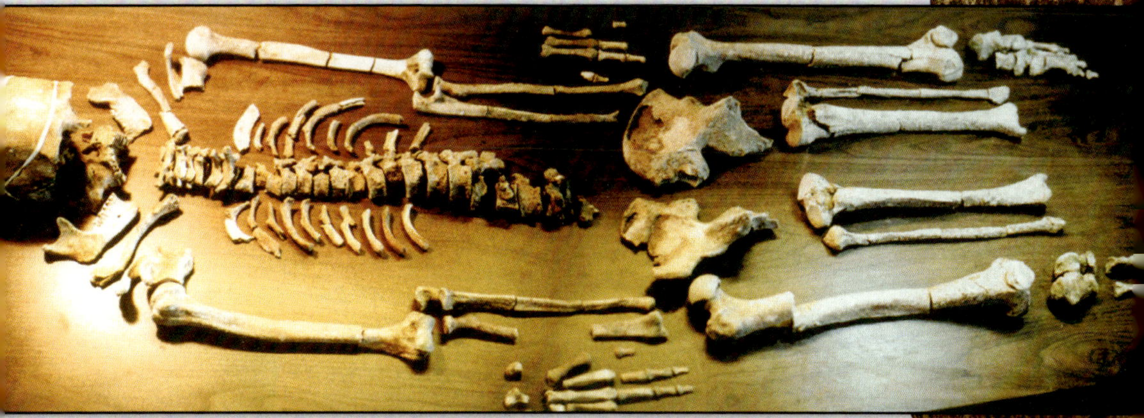

The Kennewick Man's skeleton is nearly complete, missing only a few hand and feet bones. During his life, he suffered numerous injuries including at least six fractured ribs.

thrived on a diet low in sugar and starch. Researchers also found a spearpoint stuck in his hipbone, but it was unlikely the cause of his death, and it may have been there for several years before he died. A 2015 study found that Kennewick Man is more closely related to modern Native Americans than any other living population. The origins and ownership of Kennewick Man have been hotly debated for years.

The earliest evidence for Paleoindians was found in coastal California. In 1959, Phil Orr found three human bones on Santa Rosa Island, California. He called his discovery Arlington Springs Man, after the canyon where the bones were buried 30 feet (9 m) deep. The fossils were originally thought to be ten thousand years old. But a re-evaluation done forty years later dated the bones at thirteen thousand years old. And new measurements revealed that Arlington Springs Man was actually a woman!

When Arlington Springs Woman lived on the land it was one mega island. The climate was much cooler than it is today. She may have shared the land with pygmy mammoths. Still massive in size, pygmy mammoths were at 7 feet (2 m) high at the tallest and weighed around 2,000 pounds (907 kg)—about half the size of a Columbian mammoth. Many pygmy mammoth fossils have been found on Santa Rosa Island. Some researchers also believe that Arlington Springs Woman may have arrived to the island by boat. This suggests that some early humans migrated to the Americas by watercraft. Arlington Springs Woman's bones are the oldest *Homo sapiens* fossils found to date in North America.

Chapter 6
To Be Continued . . .

Human origins and evolution are complex topics. The study of paleoanthropology is an ever-evolving science with new discoveries found all the time, all over the world. New fossil finds add to the human story, enriching the picture of our prehistoric past.

Breakthrough Roles

Recent discoveries found in the Rift Valley and in southern Africa add to the complexity. In the Hadar region of the Rift Valley, a new fossil was uncovered, and it's shaking up the early human family tree. The Ledi jaw was found in 2013, just miles from where Lucy was excavated. The jaw is dated between 2.8 and 2.7 million years old. It is thought to be from the *Homo* group. It might even be from a newly discovered species. The fossil's five intact teeth are considerably smaller

The Ledi jaw is part of a lower mandible. It was exposed by the erosion of a hillside in the Rift Valley.

than other hominin fossils found in the area. The Ledi jaw could provide insight into how the *Homo* genus evolved. But with all discoveries in paleoanthropology, the findings are first met with a critical and discerning eye. Only time and more research will tell the full story of the Ledi jaw.

Another new fossil find was uncovered deep inside a cave in South Africa. In 2013, paleoanthropologist Lee Berger and his team found a new species, *Homo naledi*, in Rising Star cave. The cave has only one entrance and is extremely difficult and dangerous to explore. Researchers had to employ an expedition team that was small enough to fit into the 7-inch-wide (18-cm) chute and climb down the 39-foot-long (12-m) chimney-like shaft. The team was nicknamed the "underground astronauts." The petite spelunkers squeezed through dark and narrow passages, often crawling on all fours to excavate the fifteen hundred fossils. They uncovered dozen of teeth, jaws, rib bones, skulls, and hand and feet bones. They found at least fifteen men and women of different ages. Because no other animal fossils were uncovered at the site, researchers believe that group was intentionally deposited. It is unusual to find that many of the same species in the same hidden spot. Did Berger and his team of underground astronauts stumble upon a graveyard? How *Homo naledi* got there is still being investigated. There are likely more bones to be excavated, too.

Homo naledi have tiny heads, with braincases half the size of modern humans'. Their bodies are more

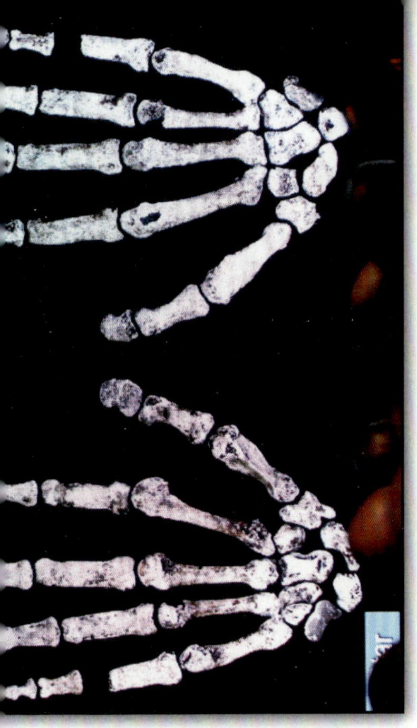

An almost complete Homo naledi *hand was excavated in the Rising Star cave.*

contemporary, with long legs, arched feet, and flattened fingertips for precise gripping. But they also have high shoulders and long, curved fingers. These are usually used for climbing and hanging in trees. It's hard to say where *Homo naledi* fits in the early human family tree. The fossils and cave sediments have not been dated yet. The bones are not only challenging to excavate from the deep chamber but also difficult to date. Unlike finds from the Rift Valley, the Rising Star bones were not buried in volcanic ash or with other fossils. They were barely submerged on a cave floor of mixed sediments. Researchers are still figuring the best and most accurate way to date the *Homo naledi* fossils.

Back to the Future

At some point you may have asked, why bother? What's the point of studying our ancient past, especially since it can be so difficult to find evidence or to accurately and absolutely date the evidence? It seems like there are more questions than answers.

The goal of paleoanthropology is to better understand our humanness. It is the study of human

Molecular Clock Dating

Molecular clock dating doesn't exactly use a wristwatch with a short hand for hours and a long hand for minutes. Instead it is a tool used to calculate the time of evolutionary events. Molecular clock dating measures the mutations in different gene sequences to figure out when two species, such as an ape and a hominin, separated to become two different animals. Looking at two stretches of DNA, scientists count the number of mutations to map out evolutionary changes over time. Molecular clock dating is good for filling in gaps when scientists have no fossil record for an animal. It's also good for organizing evolutionary events chronologically. But because DNA decays rapidly, this method doesn't work with dating really old fossils. Molecular clock dating has been around for a while, but scientists are still refining its use and continue to search for different approaches to the clock.

biology and behavior. It looks at how environmental changes affected early human growth and survival. By looking at early human fossils, researchers can search for the roots of physical traits and behavior. They can see how our bodies and brains have evolved, changed, and adapted over six million years. Scientists learn how diseases have evolved.

Geneticists can study how the evolution of genes has influenced behavior, such as aggression. By examining ancient sediments, archaeologists detect how the climate has changed. Places like the Rift Valley demonstrate how the land is still changing. Studying human origins gives us direct insight into the future of humans and the planet.

Additionally, the evidence found acknowledges humankind's similarities and collective past. With this understanding, modern society may be able to see past our differences and eradicate bigotry and racism. It may help humans realize that we all share a common past and a common future.

The Search Continues

When a new fossil is discovered, researchers often hope it may be the "missing link." There are a lot of missing links in the world of paleoanthropology. Details are murky, recent discoveries throw a curveball in the face of previous discoveries, and experts disagree and debate all the time. But because there may be a lack of data, does that mean researchers can't connect the dots? Is the absence of evidence proof that scientists have got it all wrong?

Early human fossils are extremely difficult to find. Millions or thousand of years old, many fossils do not withstand the test of time. They may be buried in unreachable places or destroyed before they can be

A group of archeology students excavate a site in the Rift Valley. Check with your local museum or University for opportunities to join a dig.

discovered. But the absence of evidence does not imply it never happened. If a tree falls in the forest when no one is around, does it make a sound? Likely the sound it makes is strong and fierce. If you scarfed down a whole plate of homemade chocolate chip cookies, does that mean Dad never baked the delicious treats? Surely the stomachache and the trail of cookie crumbs are proof enough. Society even used to think the earth was flat until they took a look at the bigger picture.

The origins of humankind are incomplete, but the fossils found give us glimpses millions of years into the past. The puzzle continues. There are still questions to be answered, but that's the exciting part—much more to discover, dig up, explore, and understand about our history. We have a lot of family photo albums to fill up with the faces and stories of our early ancient ancestors.

TIMELINE

c. 25 million years ago Plate tectonics rip apart eastern Africa, building the Rift Valley.

c. 6 million years ago Humans and chimp ancestors diverge; Millennium Man (*Orrorin tugenensis*) lives.

c. 4.4 million years ago Ardi (an *Ardipithecus ramidus*) lives in Ethiopia.

c. 4 million years ago Bipedalism becomes well developed.

c. 3.6 million years ago Hominins, most likely *Australopithecus afarensis*, make the Laetoli footprints.

c. 3.3 million years ago Lucy's Baby (an *Australopithecus afarensis*) lives in Hadar, Ethiopia.

c. 3 million years ago Lucy (an *Australopithecus afarensis*) lives in Hadar, Ethiopia.

c. 2.5 million years ago Stone toolmaking develops; the *Paranthropus* Black Skull lives in West Turkana, Kenya.

c. 1.8 million years ago *Homo erectus* expands out of Africa.

c. 1.77 million years ago The owners of the Dmanisi skulls (from the *Homo* genus) live in Dmanisi, Georgia.

c. 1.6 million years ago Turkana Boy (a *Homo erectus*) lives in West Turkana, Kenya.

c. 1 million years ago The Java Man (a *Homo erectus*) lives in Java, Indonesia.

c. 790,000 years ago Fire hearths are used for cooking, socializing, and surviving.

c. 780,000–400,000 years ago Peking Man (a *Homo erectus*) lives in China.

c. 250,000 years ago Colorful pigments are used to make paleoart.

c. 195,000 years ago The *Homo sapiens* Omo I and Omo II live in southern Ethiopia.

c. 100,000 years ago Intentional burial sites are used; burying the dead becomes a ritual.

c. 30,000 years ago Cro-Magnon (a *Homo sapiens*) lives in southwestern France.

c. 13,000 years ago Arlington Springs Woman (a *Homo sapiens*) lives on coastal California.

c. 9,000 years ago Kennewick Man (a *Homo sapiens*) lives in Washington State.

Glossary

artifact An object created by early humans.

bipedalism Habitually walking upright on two feet.

chopper A stone tool used to cut meat and marrow away from animal bones.

evolution Changes in humans, animals, and the earth and environment over time.

genus A group of closely related species.

habitat An environment area where animals and plants coexist.

hand ax A stone tool with two sharpened edges used to cut meat.

hearth A firepit lined with stones, used for cooking, heating, socializing, making tools, and warding off predators.

hominin Any species that walked upright on two feet and is closely related to humans.

omnivore Person or animal that eats plants, fruit, and meat.

paleoanthropology The study of ancient human biology, behavior, and environment.

paleoartist An illustrator, sculptor, or painter who re-creates and reconstructs scientifically accurate representations of life from the ancient past.

pigment Naturally occurring minerals in rocks that produce a variety of color.

plate tectonics The scientific theory that the earth's top layer is made up of plates that shift and move to create mountains, volcanoes, and rifts.

For More Information

Archaeological Institute of America
656 Beacon Street, 6th Floor
Boston, MA 02215
(617) 353-9361
Website: http://www.archaeological.org
The Archaeological Institute of America is dedicated to archaeological research and education.

Canadian Museum of Nature
PO Box 3443, Station D
Ottawa, ON K1P 6P4
Canada
(800) 263-4433
Website: http://www.nature.ca/en/home
The Canadian Museum of Nature offers tours, workshops, and special galleries dedicated to nature.

The Field Museum of Natural History
1400 S. Lake Shore Drive
Chicago, IL 60605
(312) 922-9410
Website: http://www.fieldmuseum.org
The Field Museum explores scientific discovery and the exploration of life on earth.

Institute of Human Origins
Arizona State University
PO Box 874101
Tempe, AZ 85287
(480) 727-6580
Website: http://www.iho.asu.edu

Institute of Human Origins is a research organization devoted to the science of human origins.

Museum of Anthropology, University of British Columbia
6393 NW Marine Drive
Vancouver, BC V6T 1Z2
Canada
(604) 827-5932
Website: http://www.moa.ubc.ca
This museum is dedicated to the education of world arts and cultures. It offers a massive online collection of cultural artifacts.

National Museum of Natural History
PO Box 37012
Smithsonian Institution
Washington DC 20013
(202) 633-1000
Website: http://www.mnh.si.edu
The National Museum of Natural History is devoted to education, discovery, and exploration of the natural world.

Websites

Because of the changing nature of Internet links, Rosen Publishing has developed an online list of websites related to the subject of this book. This site is updated regularly. Please use this link to access the list:

http://www.rosenlinks.com/FHEC/rift

For Further Reading

Anderson, Michael. *Investigating Plate Tectonics, Earthquakes, and Volcanoes*. New York, NY: Rosen Publishing, 2011.

Aronson, Marc, and Lee Berger. *The Skull in the Rock: How a Scientist, a Boy, and Google Earth Opened a New Window on Human Origins*. Washington, DC: National Geographic Children's Books, 2012.

Brooks, Philip. *The Story of Prehistoric Peoples*. New York, NY: Rosen Publishing, 2012.

Dalal, Roshen. *The Illustrated Timeline of the History of the World*. New York, NY: Rosen Publishing, 2012.

Deem, James. *Faces from the Past: Forgotten People of North America*. Boston, MA: HMH Books for Young Readers, 2012.

Diamond, Jared. *The Third Chimpanzee for Young People: On the Evolution and Future of the Human Animal.* New York, NY: Triangle Square, 2014.

Gurche, John. *Shaping Humanity: How Science, Art, and Imagination Help Us Understand Our Origins*. New Haven, CT: Yale University Press, 2013.

Henderson, Harry. *The Leakey Family: Unearthing Human Ancestors*. New York, NY: Chelsea House Publishers, 2012.

Pollard, Elizabeth, Clifford Rosenberg, and Robert Tignor. *Worlds Together, Worlds Apart: A History of the World: From the Beginnings of Humankind to the Present*. New York, NY: W. W. Norton & Company, 2015.

Prehistoric Life: The Definitive Visual History of Life on Earth. London, UK: DK Publishing, 2012.

Rubalcaba, Jill, and Peter Robertshaw. *Every Bone Tells a Story: Hominin Discoveries, Deductions, and Debates*. Watertown, MA: Charlesbridge Publishing, 2010.

Tattersall, Ian, Rob DeSalle, and Patricia Wynne. *The Great Human Journey: Around the World in 22 Million Days*. Piermont, NH: Bunker Hill Publishing Inc., 2013.

Walker, Sally, and Douglas Owsley. *Their Skeletons Speak: Kennewick Man and the Paleoamerican World*. Minneapolis, MN: Carolrhoda Books, 2012.

Woods, Mary, and Michael Woods. *Ancient Communication Technology: Sharing Information With Scrolls and Smoke Signals*. Minneapolis, MN: Twenty-First Century Books, 2011.

Woods, Mary, and Michael Woods. *Ancient Transportation Technology: From Oars to Elephants*. Minneapolis, MN: Twenty-First Century Books, 2011.

BIBLIOGRAPHY

Australia Museum. "A Timeline of Fossil Discoveries." Retrieved November 30, 2015 (http://www.australianmuseum.net.au).

Balter, Michael. "World's Oldest Stone Tools Discovered in Kenya." *Science*, April 14, 2015 (http://www.news.sciencemag.org).

Callaway, Ewen. "Teeth from China Reveal Early Human Trek Out of Africa." *Nature*, October 14, 2015 (http://www.nature.com/news/teeth-from-china-reveal-early-human-trek-out-of-africa-1.18566).

Hamilton, John. "Myth Busting: The Truth About Animals And Tools." National Public Radio, December 23, 2011 (http://www.npr.org).

Miller, Kenneth. "Archaeologists Find Earliest Evidence of Humans Cooking With Fire." *Discover Magazine*, May 2013.

Potts, Richard. *What Does It Mean to Be Human?* Washington, DC: National Geographic Books, 2010.

Shreeve, Jamie. "This Face Changes the Human Story. But How?" *National Geographic*, September 10, 2015 (http://www.news.nationalgeographic.com).

Sloan, Christopher. *The Human Story: Our Evolution from Prehistoric Ancestors*. Washington, DC: National Geographic Children's Books, 2004.

Smithsonian National Museum of Natural History. "Human Family Tree." Retrieved November 26, 2015 (http://www.humanorigins.si.edu/evidence/human-family-tree).

Smithsonian National Museum of Natural History. "Olorgesailie: Life and Times of the Handaxe Makers." Retrieved November 26, 2015 (http://www.humanorigins.si.edu/research/east-african-research/olorgesailie).

Wayman, Erin. "The Top Ten Human Evolution Discoveries from Ethiopia." *Smithsonian*, October 10, 2012 (http://www.smithsonianmag.com).

Wayman, Erin. "*Australopithecus sediba*: The Wood-Eating Hominid." *Smithsonian*, June 27, 2012 (http://www.smithsonianmag.com).

Wood, James. "East Africa's Great Rift Valley: A Complex Rift System." Retrieved November 20, 2015 (http://www.geology.com/articles/east-africa-rift.shtml).

INDEX

About the Author

Growing up in Washington, DC, Kristina Lyn Heitkamp fondly remembers spending hours in the National Museum of Natural History. She would hunt for an uncanny reflection in the paleoart. This experience motivated her to venture west, to the birthplace of her ancestors. She is a Montana-based writer, researcher, and environmental journalist. She earned a bachelor of arts in English from the University of Utah and a master of arts in environmental science and natural resource journalism from the University of Montana. Kristina is a freelance

researcher for National Geographic Books and is a contributor to the children's magazines *Odyssey*, *Muse*, and *Faces*. When she is not writing about bioprinting, zero waste, or human bones, she can be found exploring northwestern Montana with a fishing pole or hiking boots.

Photo Credits

Cover, p. 3 © iStockphoto.com/Mhgallery; pp. 7, 35 Wolfgang Kaehler/LightRocket/Getty Images; p. 10 Melville B. Grosvenor/National Geographic Image Collection/Getty Images; p. 12 © AP Images; p. 15 Nick Fox/Shutterstock.com; p. 17 De Agostini Picture Library/Getty Images; pp. 19, 31 Encyclopaedia Britannica/Universal Images Group/Getty Images; p. 21 Dave Einsel/Getty Images; p. 22 Chip Hires/Gamma-Rapho/Getty Images; pp. 26, 41 Kenneth Garrett/National Geographic Image Collection/Getty Images; p. 28 © The Natural History Museum/Alamy Stock Photo; p. 37 Anna Zieminski/AFP/Getty Images; p. 39 © Greatstock Photographic Library/Alamy Stock Photo; p. 43 Sebastien Plailly/Science Source; p. 45 Emmanuel Laurent/Science Source; p. 47 Anadolu Agency/Getty Images; p. 49 Foto24/Gallo Images/Getty Images; p. 52 Stefan Heunis/AFP/Getty Images; back cover, interior pages (rock formation) © iStockphoto.com/franckreporter; interior pages (evolution illustration) © iStockphoto.com/Xrisca30, (rocky texture) © iStockphoto.com/velkol

Designer: Matt Cauli; Editor: Amelie von Zumbusch; Photo Researcher: Bruce Donnola